Survival Secrets of Sea Animals

TEXT BY MARY JO RHODES AND DAVID HALL
PHOTOGRAPHS BY DAVID HALL

Undersea
Encounters

Children's Press®
A Division of Scholastic Inc.
New York Toronto London Auckland Sydney
Mexico City New Delhi Hong Kong
Danbury, Connecticut

Library of Congress Cataloging-in-Publication Data

Rhodes, Mary Jo, 1957–
    Survival secrets of sea animals / text by Mary Jo Rhodes and David Hall ; photographs by David Hall.
        p. cm. (Undersea encounters)
    Includes index.
    ISBN-10: 0-516-24398-5 (lib. bdg.)   0-516-25464-2 (pbk.)
    ISBN-13: 978-0-516-24398-6 (lib. bdg.)   978-0-516-25464-7 (pbk.)
    1. Marine animals—Juvenile literature. 2. Animal defenses—Juvenile literature. I. Hall, David, 1943 Oct. 2–ill. II. Title.
    QL122.2.R494 2006
    591.4709162—dc22

                            2005036408

For my daughter Jessica, who loves the small and hidden animals
of the undersea world most of all.
—D. H.

To my husband John for his encouragement and support, and for organizing trips to see
whales and sea turtles in the wild, a snorkeling adventure, and excursions to tidepools.
Without his involvement, most of my knowledge of undersea life would be from books only.
And to the memory of my father-in-law, Jack Rounds, who passed along his deep love
of nature and animals to my husband, John, and to our sons Jeremy and Tim.
—M. J. R.

All photographs © 2007 by David Hall except: Minden Pictures/Fred Bavendam: 42 right; Nature Picture Library Ltd./Constantinos Petrinos: 39 bottom.

A lionfish can deliver a painful sting.
pg. **16**

The color pattern of a young angelfish can confuse its enemies.
pg. **31**

Survival Secrets of Sea Animals

Ghost pipefish look like blades of seagrass.
pg. **27**

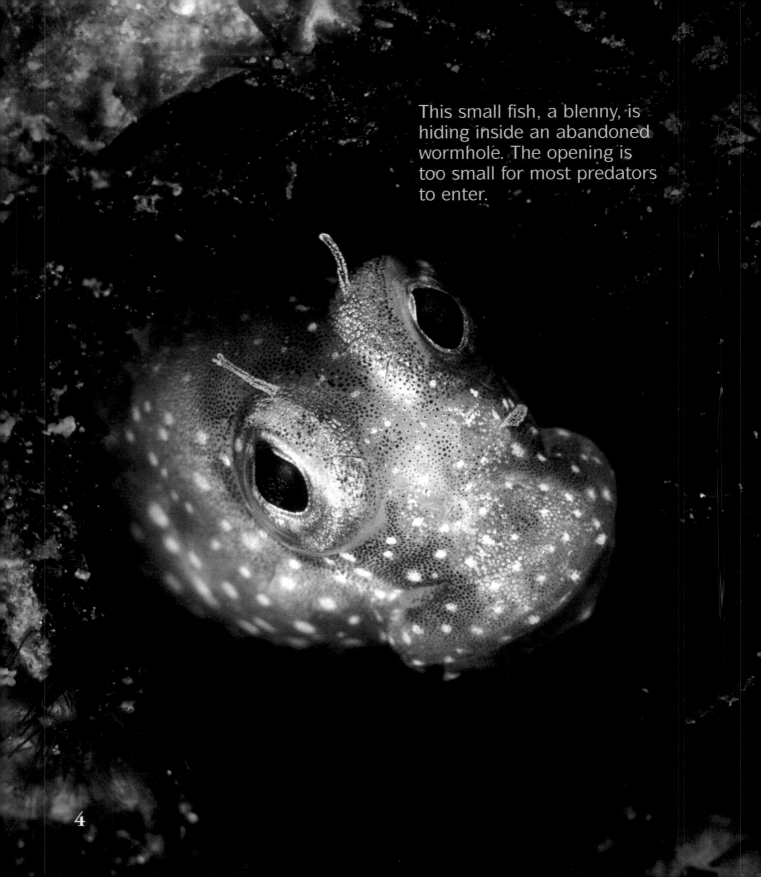

This small fish, a blenny, is hiding inside an abandoned wormhole. The opening is too small for most predators to enter.

chapter 1

A Place to Hide

Imagine for a moment that you are a small fish in the ocean. You are surrounded by larger fish with one thing on their minds—eating you for lunch! What would you do?

Every animal that lives in the sea is hunted by other animals. All sea animals must protect themselves from hungry **predators**. A safe home or hiding place is a simple and effective defense used by many small animals.

When threatened, a pikeblenny retreats tail-first into an old, abandoned wormhole.

A garden eel will retreat into its sandy burrow at the first sign of danger.

A Hole to Hide In

Any small opening on the sea bottom can be a safe place to hide. Some animals have a favorite hole, or den, where they live. Others dart into any nearby empty hole and remain there until danger has passed. An ideal hiding place is one that is too small for a predator to enter.

Digging a Burrow

Some animals construct homes for themselves on the seafloor. Garden eels and mantis shrimps (see cover photo) dig burrows in sandy sea bottoms. Garden eels don't even need to leave their homes to eat, because their food comes to them. They gobble up tiny animals that float past their burrows.

A Borrowed Home

Mollusks, such as snails, are protected by a hard shell. But what happens to the shell when a snail dies? Hermit crabs live inside the discarded shells. A

This hermit crab is living inside a shell that once belonged to a large snail called a triton.

hermit crab hides inside its borrowed shell when danger threatens. As the crab grows, it exchanges its shell for a larger one.

Buried Alive

Invertebrates are animals without backbones, such as snails, crabs, and sea stars. Many of these animals hide by burying themselves in sand or mud. Buried animals typically come up out of the sand at night, when many predators are asleep.

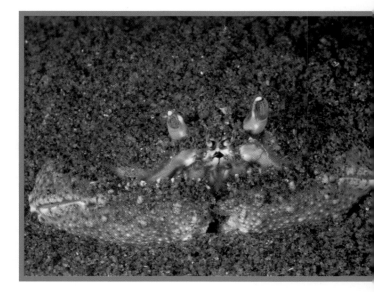

This box crab has buried itself in sand to hide from predators.

Artificial Homes

People sometimes use the ocean as a place to throw things they no longer want. This garbage spoils the beauty of the underwater environment and may contain chemicals that are harmful to sea animals. Occasionally, the discarded items are reused. Animals sometimes make their homes in old bottles, cans, or tires. A shipwreck may become an artificial reef that provides homes for many sea animals.

This fierce-looking male wolf eel is really very shy. He and his mate have made their home inside the remains of a sunken ship.

An old soda can makes
a good hiding place for
a pair of small gobies.

An old coconut shell has
become the home of a
jeweled blenny. The shell
is covered with algae
and sponges.

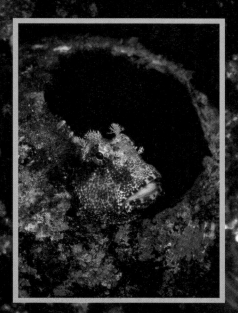

A sea star hunts
for prey inside a
discarded tin can.

A lionfish is protected by sharp, **venomous** spines in its fins. A sting from one of these spines is extremely painful.

chapter 2

Sharp Weapons

Like undersea knights, sea animals often protect themselves with sharp weapons and armor. Their sharp weapons are called **spines**. Animals that use spines for defense include sea urchins, lobsters, and many kinds of fish.

Lobsters and sea urchins also have a hard shell that is like armor. There are even fish, such as boxfish and seahorses, that have a kind of bony armor.

A sea urchin is protected by a hard outer shell and many sharp spines.

A Living Pincushion

Sea urchins are related to sea stars. They have round bodies protected by hard shells and many spines. Some urchins have dozens of long, needle-sharp spines. Others have fewer or shorter spines.

In some cases, the spines contain venom or other chemicals that can deliver a painful sting.

Small crabs or shrimps often live with sea urchins. They are safe among the urchins' spines, where predators can't reach them.

The slate pencil urchin has just a few thick spines. It uses the spines to lock itself into tight crevices so that predators can't pull it out.

A Dangerous Worm

Fireworms are invertebrate predators related to earthworms. They feed on **corals** and other animals. Fireworms are protected by bundles of needle-sharp spines that stick out from their bodies. These spines are coated with a substance that causes a severe burning sensation. Divers are careful not to touch these animals.

Fireworms look like bristle-covered earthworms, but watch out! Each needle-sharp bristle is covered with a substance that causes a very painful sting.

Armored Knights

Crabs and lobsters have a hard outer shell that is like armor. Many of them have large claws, which are powerful weapons. But most lobsters do not have large claws with which to defend themselves. Spiny lobsters have long, sharp **antennae**. When threatened, they keep their antennae pointed at an attacker, preventing it from getting too close.

Spiny lobsters defend themselves with a pair of long, stiff antennae that are used to keep an attacker away.

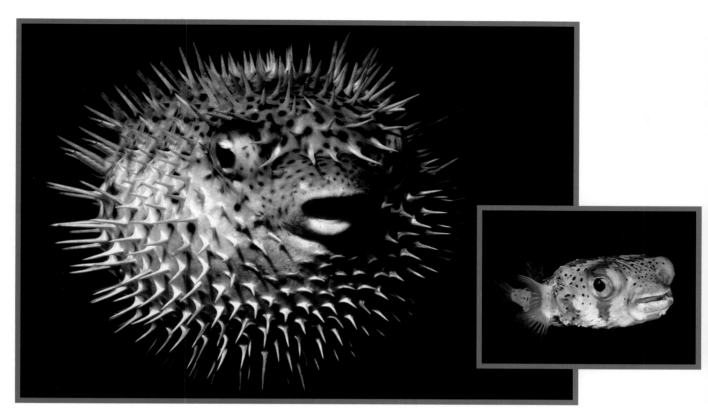

When a spiny pufferfish inflates itself by swallowing water, its sharp spines stand straight out from its body.

Pop-up Weapons

Spiny puffers, or porcupinefish, are covered with many sharp spines like a porcupine. These spines normally lie flat against the fish's body. When the puffer is frightened, it swallows a lot of water very quickly. Its body blows up like a balloon, which makes the sharp spines stick straight out.

Fish with Spines

Many fish have stiff spines in their fins, and some have additional spines. For example, a cowfish has spines on its head. Stiff spines make a fish more difficult for a predator to swallow.

Spines can protect in other ways. Scorpionfish and stingrays have venomous spines. Triggerfish have a thick spine that can be used to lock themselves into tight places.

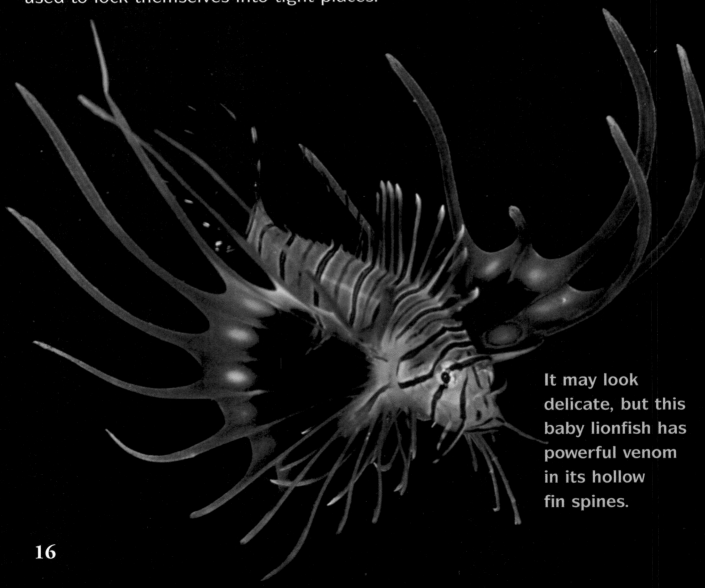

It may look delicate, but this baby lionfish has powerful venom in its hollow fin spines.

Boxfish are protected by bony armor and by bad-tasting chemicals in their skin. A cowfish is a boxfish with additional protection—spines that stick out from its head like the horns of a cow.

A filefish has a thick spine on the top of its head. The spine stands upright at the first sign of danger. This makes the fish a more difficult mouthful for a predator to bite or swallow.

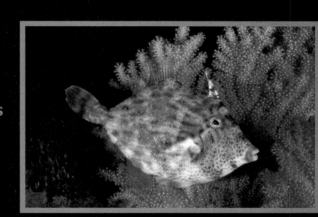

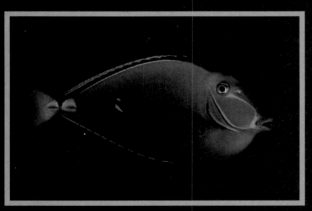

This surgeonfish has two pairs of sharp spines at the base of its tail that can be used to slash at an attacker. The surgeonfish advertises its sharp spines with a bright orange color.

The stingray has a sharp, venomous spine near the base of its tail. The ray can whip its tail up and forward, driving the stinger into a predator or a person who accidentally steps on it.

Bigeye jacks swim together in an organized group called a school. Schooling is one method that fish use to defend themselves from predators.

chapter 3

Safety in Numbers

Do you feel safer when you are with friends than when you are alone? It seems as if many fish do. Fish often swim together in groups called **schools**. A school consists of many fish, usually of the same kind, or **species**. The fish in a school are usually the same size. A school may be small with just a few fish or very large with thousands of fish. Schooling behavior helps fish survive in several ways.

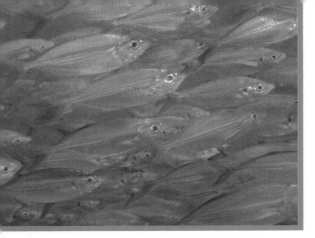

A large number of fish schooling closely together can confuse an attacker.

A large group of soldier-fish schools inside an underwater cave.

A Confusing Target

Predators such as sharks and barracudas like to pick out a single target before striking. When many fish swim and turn together as one, the predator can become confused. By schooling together, fish may avoid being attacked.

An Early Warning

Fish that school together gain another advantage. Predators like to surprise their prey. The more fish there are in a school, the less likely it is that they will be taken by surprise.

Combined Weapons

Some defenses are more effective when used by a large group of fish. Surgeonfish are named for the sharp, scalpel-like spines on their tails. A predator might easily avoid the sharp spines by attacking a single surgeonfish at its head end. But it may be more risky to attack an entire school of these well-armed fish.

The defensive spines on surgeonfish are most effective when the fish swim together.

Schooling or Shoaling?

Any group of fish hanging out together can be called a shoal. Not every shoal, however, is a school. When the shoal is organized and every fish is swimming in the

A disorganized group of feeding damselfish is a shoal but not a school.

same direction, the shoal is also a school. Fish may shoal together for feeding or mating.

Schooling Fact

At least one-quarter of all species of fish are known to school. Some kinds of fish school only when they are young and need the most protection.

21

Leaflike growths on its skin help to disguise a leafy sea dragon. When it swims among seaweeds, this seahorse relative becomes almost invisible.

22

chapter 4

The Invisible Fish

How can you be looking right at an animal and still not see it? The answer is **camouflage**. A camouflaged animal has a shape, a color, and behaviors that allow it to blend in with its surroundings. Fish and other animals use camouflage to hide from predators. Predators also use camouflage to help them catch their prey. Many animals use camouflage for both purposes at the same time.

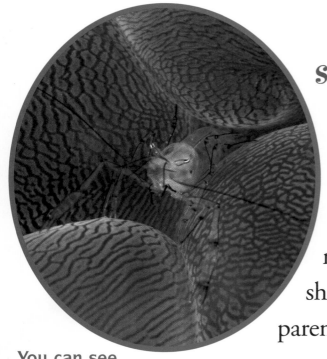

You can see through the body of this small shrimp.

See-Through Animals

Some animals are nearly invisible because their bodies are transparent. You can see right through them as if they were made of glass. Some small fish, shrimps, and jellyfish have transparent bodies.

A Disappearing Act

A filefish can be visible one moment and seem to disappear the next. It has a very thin, flat body. The filefish is easy to see from the side, but when it turns to face you, it suddenly disappears.

A green filefish is difficult to see among the seagrass, but when it turns to face a predator head-on, it seems to disappear almost completely.

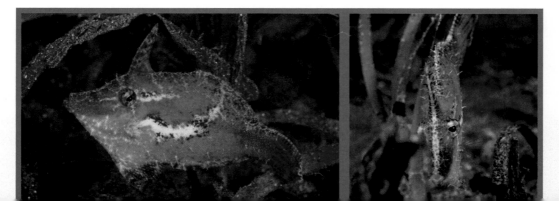

24

This flounder's body is flattened from side to side. Both of its eyes are located on the left side of its head.

Blending with the Bottom

Fish that live on the seafloor, such as flounders, crocodilefish, and scorpionfish, are experts at camouflaging themselves. They are able to change color to blend in with any combination of sand, mud, rocks, or coral. Some bottom-

The body of a crocodilefish is flattened from top to bottom. Unlike a flounder, it has one eye on the right side and one on the left.

25

The outline of this devil scorpionfish is difficult to recognize among broken bits of dead coral.

dwellers will even cover themselves with sand by wiggling their bodies back and forth while lying on the sandy bottom.

Flounders, crocodilefish, and stingrays have a flattened body shape which adds to their disguise. Most scorpionfish have small skin growths that help disguise the outline of the fish's body.

The speckled pattern of a marble ray blends in almost perfectly with the rocky seafloor below it.

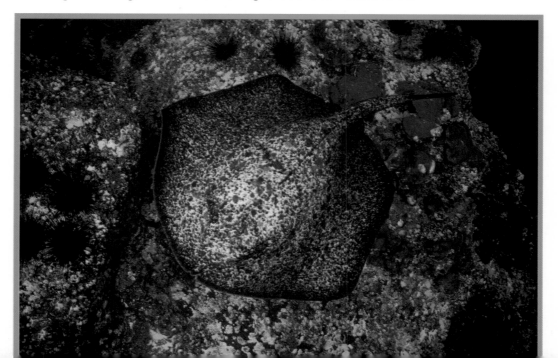

26

Hidden in the Grass

Some fish use a combination of color, shape, and behavior to imitate seagrasses. Slender razorfish and ghost pipefish swim with their heads down, imitating thin blades of grass. The color and round profile of a pygmy filefish (below) help disguise it among broad-leafed seagrasses.

A pair of green ghost pipefish imitate seagrass. ▼

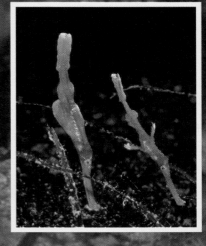

Razorfish ▶ disappear among these grass plants.

The unusual color pattern of the clown triggerfish is confusing to a predator. Is it a fish or something else? Which end is which?

chapter 5

Colors That Confuse

Camouflage colors are used to hide an animal, but other color patterns may do just the opposite. Bright colors advertise an animal by calling attention to it. Some animals are brightly colored as a warning to predators to leave them alone. Other bright colors may work to fool predators by giving them false information.

Which End Is Which?

Predators generally attack at the head end of a fish, where the eye is located.

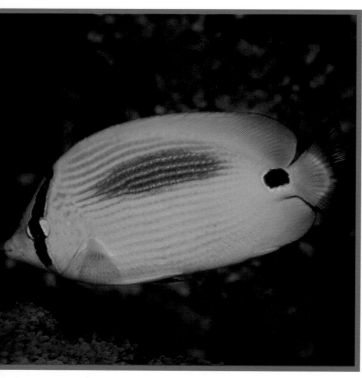

Many butterflyfish have a color pattern that disguises their eyes. This fish also has a false eye near its tail.

Butterflyfish have developed a color pattern to fool predators. They have a band of dark color that hides their eyes. Some butterflyfish also have an eye-spot near their tail end. This false eye can trick a predator into striking at the wrong place. The butterflyfish has a much better chance of escaping if a predator attacks its tail instead of its head.

A Jumble of Color

A color pattern can protect an animal by disguising the outline of its body. An example is the clown triggerfish. Its pattern of white circles on a black background creates a very confusing appearance. Young angelfish also have confusing color patterns. When they become adults and need less protection, they lose their baby colors.

The colors of a young emperor angelfish (top) confuse predators. The adult fish (bottom) looks much different but still has a pattern that disguises its eyes.

Warning Colors

Some animals display warning colors when they are threatened. Scorpionfish are camouflaged predators with venom in their fin spines. When they are disturbed, scorpionfish may spread their fins to display bright colors. An attacker that ignores this warning will receive a painful sting.

The Caledonian stinger is a scorpionfish with venom in its spines.

▲ When the Caledonian stinger is disturbed, it spreads its fins wide and displays bright warning colors.

The twinspot goby uses false eyespots to frighten away predators. Some people believe that the eyespots and jerky movements of the fish mimic the appearance of a crab.

chapter 6

Copycat Defenses

An animal may trick predators into believing that it has strong defenses. It does this by copying the appearance of a different animal. This copycat is called a **mimic**, and the animal it copies is called the model. The model is usually a poisonous or bad-tasting animal with bright colors that warn predators to stay away. A successful copycat mimics its model with color, shape, and behavior.

Flatworm or Flatfish?

Flatworms are small, colorful animals with bad-tasting chemicals in their bodies. Their colors warn predators that they are not good to eat. A few small fish take advantage of this situation by copying the color pattern of a flatworm.

One kind of fish, a tiny flounder, mimics the gliding movement of a flatworm over a sandy bottom. The young pinnate batfish mimics the appearance of a swimming flatworm.

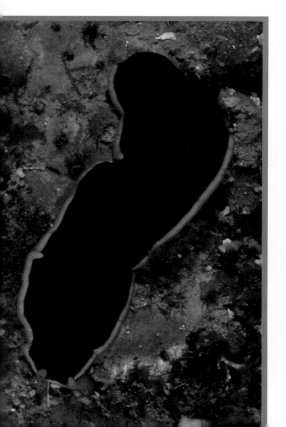

A tiny flounder (middle) and a young batfish (right) mimic the appearance of a bad-tasting flatworm (left).

A Fake Puffer

The black-saddled toby is a small pufferfish. It does not have sharp spines, but its skin and organs contain poison. Predators learn to leave this fish alone.

The mimic leatherjacket is not poisonous. It is a filefish that copies the toby's colors almost perfectly. In some cases, the disguise is so good that you can tell the two apart only by the shape of their transparent fins.

The black-saddled toby (top) is a small pufferfish. The leatherjacket (bottom) mimics the appearance of the poisonous toby so predators leave it alone.

The Copy Catfish

Striped ocean catfish have sharp spines that contain venom. These fish always swim in schools, and few predators would dare to attack them.

The convict blenny is another schooling fish. It has a similar striped pattern and is sometimes called the false catfish. False catfish look a lot like real catfish, but they do not have venomous spines. False catfish are usually safe from attack because predators mistake them for the real thing.

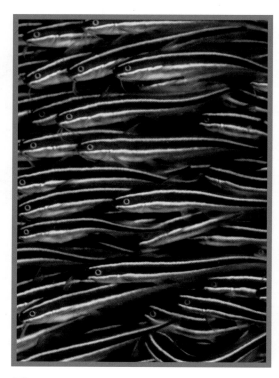

These schooling striped catfish have venomous spines and predators rarely attack them.

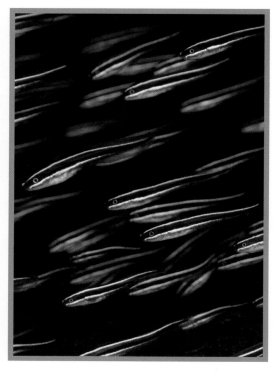

False catfish do not have venom, but their resemblance to real catfish fools most predators.

The Mimic Octopus

Octopuses are masters of disguise. They can change shape and color quickly. Most octopuses are experts at blending in with their surroundings. The mimic octopus uses a different defense. It changes its shape in what appears to be an attempt to copy the appearance of other animals. When threatened it may mimic animals with strong defenses, such as stingrays or venomous sea snakes.

To discourage predators a mimic octopus may copy the appearance of other animals, such as sea snakes (above) or a stingray (below).

Copycat Fact

Copycat defenses work best when the model animal is more common than the one that mimics it. When there are too many mimics, predators may not be fooled.

Small animals without strong defenses sometimes live with partners for protection. This clownfish is protected by the stinging ability of its **sea anemone** partner.

chapter 7

More Survival Secrets

Sea animals defend themselves in many more ways. Here are just a few examples.

Regeneration

Sea stars have an unusual survival secret. If a predator tears off one of the animal's arms, it will grow a new one in a few months. This is called **regeneration**. Not only will the sea star grow a new arm, but the arm that was torn off may also grow into a whole new sea star!

This sea star has regenerated itself from a single arm that was torn off by a predator.

Sea cucumbers defend themselves by expelling a sticky inner organ that looks like spaghetti.

Sea cucumbers are related to sea stars. They look like giant, fat worms. If a sea cucumber is attacked, it may eject one of the organs from inside its body. The material ejected is sticky and tastes bad. Like its sea star cousins, the sea cucumber will later regenerate the lost parts.

A Shocking Defense

Electric rays have a pair of organs on either side of their head that can produce as much as 200 volts of electricity. This is enough to deliver a powerful shock. Electric rays use this ability for defense and also to stun their prey.

An electric ray protects itself by delivering a powerful electric shock.

Stolen Weapons

Nudibranchs are related to snails but have no shell. Some nudibranchs prey on **hydroids** and other stinging animals. They eat these animals without getting stung. The stingers are not digested but instead travel to white growths on the nudibranch's back. The stingers can then be used to defend the nudibranch from other predators!

Every kind of sea animal has its own ways of defending itself against predators. Every predator has its own methods of catching prey. Learning about predation and defense helps us understand the delicate balance of life in the ocean.

A pink nudibranch feeds on stinging hydroids.

Glossary

antennae (**an-TEN-ee**) movable sense organs on the head of lobsters, crabs, and related animals *(pg. 14)*

camouflage (**KAM-uh-flahzh**) the blending in of an animal with its surroundings *(pg. 23)*

corals (**KOR-uhls**) small invertebrate animals that live together in groups, or colonies; some corals build large limestone structures called coral reefs *(pg. 13)*

hydroids (**HYE-droyds**) stinging animals related to corals, sea anemones, and jellyfish *(pg. 43)*

invertebrates (**in-VUR-tuh-brits**) animals with no backbone or inner skeleton; jellyfish, crabs, sea stars, worms, and snails are invertebrates *(pg. 7)*

mimic (**MIM-ick**) an animal that copies the appearance and behavior of another animal *(pg. 35)*

mollusks (**MOL-uhsks**) soft-bodied invertebrate animals that are often protected by a hard shell; snails, clams, scallops, sea slugs, octopuses, and squids are mollusks *(pg. 7)*

nudibranchs (**NOO-duh-branks**) mollusks that are related to snails but have no outer shell *(pg. 43)*

predators (**PRED-uh-turz**) animals that hunt and kill other animals for food *(pg. 5)*

prey (**PRAY**) an animal that is killed and eaten by another animal *(pg. 9)*

regeneration (**ree-JEN-uh-RAY-shun**) the process of growing back a lost body part *(pg. 41)*

schools (**SKOOLZ**) organized shoals of fish that move and turn together as one *(pg. 19)*

sea anemone (**SEE uh-NEM-uh-nee**) invertebrate animal with tentacles that are covered with stingers *(pg. 40)*

species (**SPEE-seez**) a particular kind of animal or plant *(pg. 19)*

spines (**SPINES**) stiff, sharp-pointed structures used by animals and plants for protection *(pg. 11)*

venomous (**VEN-uhm-us**) filled with poison that can be delivered into the body of an animal with a bite or sting *(pg. 10)*

Learn More About Survival Secrets of Sea Animals

Books

Kaner, Etta, and Pat Stephens (illustrator). *Animal Defenses: How Animals Protect Themselves.* Tonawanda, N.Y.: Kids Can Press, 1999.

Rhodes, Mary Jo, and David Hall. *Partners in the Sea.* Danbury, Conn.: Children's Press, 2005.

Rhodes, Mary Jo, and David Hall. *Predators of the Sea.* Danbury, Conn.: Children's Press, 2006.

Whitehouse, Patricia. *Hiding in a Coral Reef.* Chicago: Heinemann Library, 2001.

Web Sites

Crazy Camouflage
(http://www.amnh.org/education/resources)

Staying Alive
(http://magma.nationalgeographic.com/ngexplorer/0503/games/game_intro.html)

Survival Skills of Deep-Sea Animals
(http://www.mbayaq.org/efc/efc_mbh/dsc_about_survival.asp)

Index

About the Authors

After earning degrees in zoology and medicine, **David Hall** has worked for the past twenty-five years as both a wildlife photojournalist and a physician. David's articles and photographs have appeared in hundreds of calendars, books, and magazines, including *National Geographic, Smithsonian, Natural History,* and *Ranger Rick*. His underwater images have won many major awards including *Nature's Best*, BBC Wildlife Photographer of the Year, and Festival Mondial de l'Image Sous-Marine. To see more of David's work, visit www.seaphotos.com.

Mary Jo Rhodes received her M.S. in Library Service from Columbia University and was a librarian for the Brooklyn Public Library. She later worked for ten years in children's book publishing in New York City. Mary Jo lives with her husband, John Rounds, and two teenage sons, Jeremy and Tim, in Hoboken, New Jersey. To learn more about Mary Jo Rhodes and her books, visit www.maryjorhodes.com.

About the Consultants

Karen Gowlett-Holmes is an expert on the classification of marine invertebrates. She has worked as Collection Manager of Marine Invertebrates for the South Australia Museum and for the Australian scientific research organization, CSIRO. Karen has published more than forty scientific papers.

Gene Helfman is an expert on the behavior and ecology of fishes. He is a professor of ecology at the University of Georgia where he teaches ichthyology and conservation biology. Gene is the author of more than fifty scientific papers and first author of the widely used textbook *The Diversity of Fishes*.